ALWAYS VICTORIOUS!
THE EARLIEST CHURCH NOT PRE- BUT POSTMILLENNIAL

by

Rev. Prof. Dr. Francis Nigel Lee

Th.D., Ph.D., D.Min., S.T.D., D.R.E., D.Ed., D.Hum., D.Jur., D.C.L., D.Litt., D.Phil.

Caldwell-Morrow Lecturer in Church History

at the

QUEENSLAND PRESBYTERIAN THEOLOGICAL COLLEGE

BRISBANE, AUSTRALIA, 2000

This edition published January 2006 by

Bexley Christian Publications

For a list of all our available, and forthcoming publications, visit

http://www.bexleypublications.co.uk

or send an email to:

catalogue@bexleypublications.co.uk

ABOUT THE AUTHOR

Francis Nigel Lee was born in 1934 in the Westmorland County of Cumbria (in Great Britain). He is the great-grandson of a fiery preacher whose family disintegrated when he backslid. Though Lee's father was an Atheist, he married a Roman Catholic who raised her son in that faith.

At the onset of the Second World War, Lee's father was appointed by the Royal Navy as Chief Radar Officer (South Atlantic). So the family then moved to South Africa. There, Lee became a Calvinist; had the great joy of leading both of his parents to Christ; and then became a Minister of God's Word and Sacraments in the Dutch Reformed Church of Natal.

Preacher, Theologian, Lawyer, Educationist, Historian, Philosopher and Author, Lee has produced more than 330 publications (including many books) -- and also a multitude of long unpublished manuscripts.

Apart from an honorary LL.D., he has 21 earned degrees -- including eleven earned doctorates for dissertations in Education, Law, Literature, Philosophy and Theology.

Lee rises early; reads God's Word in ten languages; then walks a couple of miles before breakfast. He has been round the World seven times; has visited 110 countries (several repeatedly); and also every Continent (except Antarctica). He is in demand as a Promoter of Doctoral Students in Australia, England, Germany,

South Africa and the United States. He has also lectured and/or preached in all of those countries, as well as in Brazil, Scotland, Korea, Japan, Namibia, New Zealand, and Zambia.

Lee now lives in the Commonwealth of Australia -- where he was for twenty years the Professor of Systematic Theology and Caldwell-Morrow Lecturer in Church History at the Queensland Presbyterian Theological College. He retired in 2000.

ALWAYS VICTORIOUS!

THE EARLIEST CHURCH NOT PRE- BUT POSTMILLENNIAL

(1) Many modern Pretribulationists and other Dispensationalists (such as John Walvoord and Hal Lindsey) claim that **most** (if not **all**) of the first Early Church Fathers were **Rapturists**. Such believe Jesus could return "**any** moment" to **resurrect dead Christians** and then secretly "rapture" His dwindling though still-living Church "up in the air" **before** "the great tribulation" of ungodly earthlings. Thereafter, the Church would then return and rule with Christ on Earth for a thousand years - until God would **resurrect the wicked dead**.

(2) That notion (called "Chiliasm") is false. Neither the Church of the Older Testament (even when under foreign domination) nor the always-struggling and often-persecuted Church of the Newer Testament (even till the fourth century) ever expected to dwindle or to be whisked away; but only **to conquer this great planet Earth** under her **victorious Messiah**. That Church expected God not to the **rapture** her - but to **heal** the World His Son had come to **save**.

(3) During the fourth century, the Church's expectations and efforts were partially realized at the nominal **christianization** of the Pagan Roman Empire. For the **victory-orientated** Church of the first four centuries was overwhelmingly anti-chiliastic, and totally antipretribulationistic.

(4) Even the famous **Premillennial** Scholar Prof. George Eldon Ladd insists against Pretribulationism that "**every** Church Father who deals with this subject, expects the **Church** to **suffer** at the hands of

Antichrist.... We can find **no trace of Pretribulationism in the Early Church**. And no modern Pretribulationist has successfully proved that this particular doctrine was held by **any** of the Church Fathers or Students of the Word before the **nineteenth** century."[1]

(5) There is **no trace at all** of **Dispensationalistic Pretribulationism** in the Early Church Fathers. Neither is there any trace of it in later Church History, prior to the sudden occurrence of the 'tongues-speaking' Irvingites around A.D. 1830. See the Premillennialist Dave MacPherson's books: *The Unbelievable Pre-Trib Origin* (1973); *The Late Great Pre-Trib Rapture* (1974); and *The Incredible Cover-Up: The True Story of the Pre-Trib Rapture* (1975).

(6) Only **after** 1830 was this novel pretribulationistic eschatology speedily disseminated. This was done in Britain by the Plymouth Brethrenist J.N. Darby. It was thereafter done especially in the United States by C.I. Scofield, D.L. Moody, and L.S. Chafer - and by dispensationalistic Seminaries such as Dallas (Texas) and Grace (Indiana). But it was disseminated **only minimally** outside of those **circles** (and particularly **outside of Britain and the United States** right down to our present time).

(7) The Bible does, of course, teach the future physical catching up in the air of the saints **at the Second Coming of Christ** in Final Judgment. Matthew 24:31-40 *cf.* First Thessalonians 4:13-17. Yet the Bible does **not** teach the "**chiliastic**" idea of a "double resurrection." For the idea that a future physical "rapture" of the living saints (right after a physical resurrection of the dead saints) would be followed by a thousand-years-long visible reign of Christ Himself here on this Earth prior to the physical resurrection of the wicked dead - is unknown to Holy Scripture.

(8) Sometimes attempts are made to establish this extra-Biblical teaching - by appealing to the solitary and difficult-to-understand passage Revelation 20:3-7. But the teaching of Chiliasm is not at all derived from the Bible. Instead, it is derived from **Babel** - *via* pagan Zoroastrianism. See (18)ff.

(9) The chiliastic "double resurrection" teaching - the doctrine of two millennially separated physical resurrections - is foreign to Holy Scripture. **Pessimistic** "Chiliasm" is the very opposite of the **optimistic** doctrine of a future "**Golden Age**" of spiritual and physical prosperity on Earth - some time between the present and the resurrection of all mankind at the Final Judgment.

(10) "Chiliasm" and the future "Golden Age Millennium" **preclude** one another. Seventh day Adventists are chiliastic; and they **reject** a "Golden Age Millennium" here on Earth prior to the Final Judgment. Conversely, the **anti-chiliastic** 1658 Calvinian *Savoy Declaration* (26:4f) of Britain's Puritan Congregationalists - expects '**an earthly Golden Age**' at some future time before Christ's visible return at the **simultaneous** resurrection of **all** flesh.

(11) Now the **Older Testament** - just like the later Puritans who believed it – clearly teaches that the (**first**) advent of the Messiah[2] would be followed (sooner or later) by **a long period of prosperity** (of undeclared length), right here on Earth.[3] Moreover, this prosperous period would occur **prior** to the simultaneous[4] physical resurrection of the godly dead and the wicked dead - right before the Final Judgment.[5]

(12) Between the times of the Older Testament and the Newer Testament of the same Covenant of Grace, the Israelitic ***Apocrypha* and *Pseudepigrapha*** similarly teach that the then-prophesied soon advent of the Messiah[6] would **in due course** be followed by long lasting earthly blessings.[7] During that time, Satan would be bound.[8] That time of binding would in turn itself be succeeded by the contemporaneous physical resurrection of the blessed dead and the wicked dead.[9] For both the blessed dead and the wicked dead would be resurrected unto judgment, right prior to the inauguration of the eternal state.[10]

(13) Also the **Newer Testament** (including Revelation chapter twenty) says that Christ's Messianic reign will constantly **increase** toward a 'Golden Age.' That reign commenced at His first advent, with His incarnation and His earthly preaching of the Kingdom of God.[11] And that realm got underway especially at His resurrection from the dead and His ascension and heavenly session.[12]

(14) Since then, His reign has been expanding continually. It will keep on effecting glorious improvements to the condition of the Earth and its various inhabitants - until it brings blessings World-wide.[13] Then, a "thousand years" after that - thus Revelation chapter twenty - Christ will simultaneously resurrect[14] the dead saints and the wicked dead unto their final reward or punishment at the end of History.[15]

(15) Thus, Revelation chapter twenty's "**first** resurrection" - refers to the **spiritual** awakening of the **elect,** whenever they are regenerated by the Gospel-preaching of the Kingdom of God.[16] And Revelation chapter twenty's "living again" of the "**rest** of the dead" refers to the **physical** resurrection of the **wicked**, at the time when **all** the dead will physically be resurrected **simultaneously**. That physical resurrection will be for the purpose of administering rewards or punishments at the Final Judgment[17] - right prior to the commencement of the eternal state.[18]

(16) Moreover, **not even one** of the books of the so-called ***New Testament Apocrypha*** - which are often highly eschatological, and which frequently refer to Holy Scripture and to various doctrines of the Early Christian Church - ever advocated the chiliastic "two resurrections" theory. The plain truth is: Chiliasm is neither Old-Testamentical, Ancient- Apocryphal, Pseudepigraphical, New-Testamentical, Neo-Apocryphal, or Early-Patristic. Instead, it is a Mid-Patristic **minority viewpoint** - derived from **Zoroastrian Paganism**.

(17) Where, then, did the unscriptural chiliastic teaching of the "double resurrection" come from? Whence arose this teaching of a physical resurrection of the saints **separated** by a thousand years from a subsequent physical resurrection of the wicked? Not from the Bible - but from **Babel**!

(18) Bavinck and **Hoekstra** trace this teaching back to the ancient pagan religions of Babylon and Persia.[19] From **Babylon**, it would seem, the doctrine spread into **Persia** - giving rise to **Zoroastrian Chiliasm**. Then, centuries later, through the agency of Oriental religions such as **Mithraism** and **Mandaeism** and **Manichaeism** then prevalent in the Roman Empire - the teaching began to influence the thinking even of some of the Christians in the West.

(19) This was the case especially in pseudo-glossolalic **Phrygia** among the many heterodox and 'tongues-speaking' Montanists or Proto-Pentecostalists - from the middle of the second century of the Christian era onward. Sadly, this was also the case regarding the eschatology of the non-glossolalic and largely-orthodox Justin Martyr and Irenaeus – whose views even in other theological areas (such as soteriology, sacramentology and ecclesiology) were somewhat tinged with errors[20] (of which they themselves seem to be unaware).

(20) During the three hundred years **before** the Christian Era - the **B.C. Israelites** had lived **closer** to the Bible! **No** traces of a **chiliastic** doctrine of two widely-separated physical "double resurrections" can be found in **their** writings **then** - until some of the Israelites **judaized** by rejecting Jesus the Christ of the Bible, in favour of themselves as a false-christ from Babel.

(21) Now even the post-apostolic so-called "Christian Chiliasm" of Justin Martyr and Irenaeus had nothing to do with the idea of the arrival of a future **earthly Golden Age**. The latter was clearly revealed even from the **beginning** of God's dealings with man.[21] For the Pre-Christian **pagan** ideas of a (Messianic) Golden Age,[22] are but (perverted) **remnants** of God's **original revelation** to all men prior to the Great Flood and the Great Dispersion from the Tower of Babel onward. And those remnants were subsequently kept alive by God's **continuing revelations**, in various ways, to all men.[23]

(22) It was only from the middle of the second century A.D. onward, then, that the Babylonian-Persian **chiliastic** idea of two widely-separated physical resurrections began to expand even on the fringes of the **Christian Church**. First it influenced Sub-Christian groups like the Cerinthians, Ebionites, and the Montanists - *cf.* too the modern Mormons, Pentecostalists, Seventh-day Adventists, and Jehovah's Witnesses.[24] And then it ultimately influenced even some of the authentically-Christian groups themselves.

(23) The first authentically-Christian thinker writtenly to advocate a kind of "Chiliasm" was Justin Martyr the Samaritan. This was around 150 A.D. Yet even Justin **only sometimes** advocated a "Christian Chiliasm" - and indeed a kind of "Chiliasm" quite unlike that of modern Premillennialists.[25]

(24) Moreover, Justin always acknowledged that **Chiliasm** was always only one of a number of opinions among those early Christians - noting that "**many** who belong to the pure and pious Faith, and are True Christians, think **other-wise**."[25] This means he did not regard his own chiliastic opinion as a test of orthodoxy, but freely admitted that "**many**" of "the pure and pious" among the "**True Christians**" think "**otherwise**." Certainly there is **no** trace of Chiliasm among "True Christians" **before** Justin in any of the words of **John the Baptizer**, **Jesus**, any of the **Apostles**, the **Apostolic Fathers**, or the **Earliest Apologists** - all of whom seem to have been **Postmillennialists**.[26]

(25) Thus ***The Teaching of the Twelve Apostles*** alias the ***Didachee*** reminds both God and Christians around A.D. 97: "Let Your **Church** be gathered together from the **ends** of the Earth! ... Remember, Lord, Your **Church**..., and assemble it from the **four winds**! ... For this is that which was spoken by the Lord: '**In every place** and time, offer to Me a pure sacrifice! For...My Name shall be wonderful among the **nations**.'" Malachi 1:11-14.

(26) Also the ***Epistle of Barnabas*** around A.D. 98 declares: "The Scripture says concerning **us** [Genesis 1:28]...: 'Multiply and **fill** the Earth! ... Have **dominion** over it!' ... **We**, having been quickened and being kept alive by the faith of the promise and by the World, shall live, **ruling** over the **Earth**.... To govern implies authority, so that one **should** command and **rule**.... Christ was the Son of David.... He says [Psalm 110], 'The Lord said to my Lord, "You must keep on sitting at My right hand, until I make Your enemies Your footstool!"' And again, this is what Isaiah [45:1f] says: 'The Lord said to Christ, "My Lord Whose right hand I have held so that **the nations** shall yield obedience before Him!"'"

(27) Clement of Rome about A.D. 99 enjoins the godly: "Let us hasten with all energy...to perform **every** good work! For the Creator...formed man...and said: '**Increase** and multiply!' We see, then, how all righteous men have been adorned with good works.... Let us without delay accede to His will, and let us work the work of righteousness with our whole strength! ... Concerning His Son, the Lord spoke thus...: 'I will give You **the nations** for Your inheritance, and the **uttermost** parts of the **Earth** for Your possession.... You must keep on sitting at My right hand, until I make Your enemies Your footstool!' [Psalms 2 & 110].... Let **us** then, men and brethren, with all energy - act the part of **soldiers**, in accordance with **His Holy Commandments**!"

(28) Also the ***Pastor of Hermas*** wrote around A.D. 100: "**Increase** and **build up** and **rule over the whole creation**! ... The building...**will** be finished.... **When** the tower is **finished** and built - **then** comes the **end**.... I was met by a Beast of such a size that it could destroy peoples [Revelation 13:3f]. But through the power of the Lord and His great mercy, I escaped from it.... It will be possible for **you** to escape it, if your heart be pure...and you spend the rest of the days of your life in serving the Lord.... Cast your cares upon the Lord, and He **will** direct them! Trust the Lord! ... For He is **all**-powerful!"

(29) Ignatius said in 107: "**Victory** over death was obtained in Christ.... **Stand firm**, like an anvil which is beaten! It is the part of a noble athlete to be wounded - and **yet** to **conquer**! ... Run your race with **increasing** energy! Weigh the times carefully! While you are here, be a **conqueror**!"

(30) The ***Epistle to Diognetus*** declared about 130: "The Christians, though subjected day by day to punishment, **increase** the **more** in number.... Do you not see them exposed to the wild beasts so that they may be persuaded to deny the Lord? And yet, **they are not overcome**! Do you not see that the **more** of them who are punished, the **greater** becomes the number of the **rest**? This does not seem to be the work of man. This is **the power of God**!"

(31) Papias, who flourished around 145, was a Disciple of that very great Postmillennialist, the Apostle John[27] - who wrote his non-dispensationalistic Gospel (John 5:24-26) and his Book of Revelation (20:1-15). Papias never advocated the chiliastic doctrine of the "double resurrections" - although both he and Barnabas did, of course, refer to the different and Scriptural doctrine of the Earth's **future Golden Age**.[28] In actual fact, both Barnabas and Papias were - in the technical sense - not Premillennialists but **Postmillennialists** (alias **Consistent** "Amillennialists"). See (61)ff.

(32) The A.D. 150 **Justin Martyr**, then, was the first 'Christian Chiliast' - at least occasionally, in some of his writings. Now it must be remembered that, before his conversion, he had been a Samaritan. The Samaritans had an unorthodox Theology, which they had derived in part from the Pagans near Assyria and Babylonia, the matrix of Chiliasm. Second Kings 17:24f and Ezra 4:1f & 9:1f *cf.* John 4:9-22. Some of those views may well have carried over into an 'Occasional Chiliasm' in Justin - even after his conversion to the Christian phase of his life.

(33) Justin's 'Occasional Chiliasm' *sui generis* - which was strongly antipretribulationistic - was followed possibly by Pothinus in A.D. 175 and more probably (around 185) by Irenaeus.[29] Around 220, there were **some** similar influences on Tertullian - though only with very important and extremely **optimistic** (if not perhaps even **postmillennial** modifications and implications).30 On the other hand, 'Christian Chiliastic' ideas were indeed advocated in 240 by Commodian; in 250 by the Egyptian Bishop Nepos in his *Refutation of Allegorists*; in 260 by the almost unknown Coracion; and in 310 by Lactantius.

(34) It is true these few Christian leaders did advocate the chiliastic teaching of "two resurrections." Yet they differed from most modern Premillennialists in many ways. For they denied that, since Calvary, the Jews are in any way "God's Chosen People." They also denied it was predicted the Jews would return to Palestine. And they were all **antipretribulationistic**.

(35) Justin Martyr, for instance, believed that the **Gentile** Christians would ultimately live in Jerusalem. Irenaeus was an **Anti-Judaistic** Covenant Theologian.

Tertullian expected a **massive World-wide conversion of the Gentiles** prior to the millennium.[30] The premillennial views of Bishop Nepos were **grossly materialistic**. Commodian believed in the establishment of the New Jerusalem **before** the millennium. And Lactantius (who frequently quoted from **pagan** sources to support his views) believed that the Non-Christian Gentiles would be **enslaved** during the thousand years. What modern Dispensationalist would agree with any of these views?

(36) Justin Martyr also preserved many of the emphases of the **Postmillennialism** of the Christian Church **before** his time. Thus he taught[31] "that the **Gentiles would repent**.... The prophecy of Micah [4:1f]...is as follows: 'In the last days, the mountain of the Lord shall be manifest, established on the top of the mountains. It shall be exalted above the hills, and people shall flow unto it. And **many nations** shall go and say: "Come, let us go up to the mountain of the Lord and to the House of the God of Jacob!"'.... For it is plain that - though beheaded and crucified and and thrown to wild beasts and chains and fire and all other kinds of torture, **we do not give up** our confession! But the more such things happen - the **more** others and in **larger** numbers become faithful, and worshippers of God through the Name of Jesus."

(37) Very significantly, there is no Chiliasm whatsoever in Justin's *Fragments of the Lost Work of Justin in the Resurrection*. Indeed, even in the main thrust of his *locus classicus* on Chiliasm within his *Dialogue with Trypho* the chiliazed Judaist, Justin simply says: "There will be a resurrection of the dead.... In short, the **eternal resurrection** and judgment of **all** men would likewise take place."[25]

(38) The A.D. 165 **Tatian** was strongly anti-premillennialistic. Thus he insisted:[32] "**We** believe that there will be a resurrection of bodies **after** the consummation of all things.... A resurrection **once and for all**, when our periods of existence are completed - and in consequence solely of the constitution of things under which men alone live, **for the purpose of passing judgment** upon them!"

(39) The A.D. 183 Apologist **Athenagoras** is clearly anti-chiliastic. "It is not our belief alone," he argues,[33] "that bodies will raise again.... Many Philosophers also hold the same view.... Nothing hinders according to Pythagoras and Plato, that when the dissolution of bodies takes place - they should from the very same elements of which they were constructed at first, be reconstructed.... All human beings who die, rise again.... All are to rise again - those who have died in infancy, as well as others."

(40) "It will be well to prove our proposition by...the reward **or** punishment due to each man, in accordance with righteous judgment.... Man must also bear the recompense [due] for the sins committed...such as adultery, murder, theft, rapine, dishonour to parents, and every desire in general that tends to the injury and loss of our neighbours.... There must by all means be a resurrection of the bodies which are dead.... The **reward** or **punishment** of lives ill or well spent, is proportioned to the merit of each."

(41) Only in **some** parts of his writings, does the A.D. 185 **Irenaeus** lean toward the erroneous "two resurrections" teaching of Chiliasm.[34] Elsewhere, he rightly seems to be arguing in favour of **one simultaneous physical resurrection of both the**

godly and the wicked. Thus in his *Against Heresies*, he writes[35] that Christ "Himself declares: 'The **hour** shall come, in which **all** the dead who are in the **tombs** shall hear the voice of the Son of man and **shall come forth**; those who have done **good** to the resurrection of life, and those that have done **evil** to the resurrection of judgment' [John 5:28]."

(42) Yet again, Irenaeus seems to acknowledge that the "**first** resurrection" is purely **spiritual**; and only what some term the '**second** resurrection' is **physical**. "This," he insists, "is what the Lord declared: '**Happy** are those servants whom the Lord, when He comes, shall find watching' [Luke 12:37f].... Again, John also says **the very same** in the Apocalypse: 'Blessed and holy is he who has part in the **first** resurrection' [Revelation 20:6].... '**After** these things, the Lord shall remove **us** men far away - and **those who** remain **shall multiply upon the Earth**' [Isaiah 6:11]."

(43) Now "all these and other words," explains the **Anti-Pretribulationist** Irenaeus, "were unquestionably spoken in reference to the **resurrection** of the **just** - which takes place **after** the coming of Antichrist...in [the times of] which [resurrection] the **righteous** shall reign on the Earth...[with respect to] those whom the Lord shall find in the flesh awaiting Him from Heaven, and **who have suffered tribulation** as **well** as **escaped** the hands of the wicked one." Indeed, in a fragment of Irenaeus preserved in the *Parallela* of John of Damascus,[36] one even reads "that [our] bodies also do rise again" and "that to **each** body its own soul shall be restored.... It shall not receive bodies diverse from what they had been" but rather "as they departed this life - in sins **or** in **righteous actions**.... Such as...were in **un**belief... shall...faithfully be **judged**." Where **here** is there **any** teaching about "**two** resurrections"?!

(44) Wrote **Clement of Alexandria** in A.D. 190, quite anti-chiliastically: "The word of our Teacher [Jesus Christ] did not remain in Judea **alone**.... But it was diffused over **the whole World**, over **every** nation and village and town - already bringing whole houses over to the truth.... Our doctrine at its very first proclamation was prohibited by kings and tyrants.... But it **flourishes** the **more**.... The Father of our Lord, by the resurrection of Jesus Christ...according to your faith, **rises again** in **us**.... In the resurrection, the soul returns to the body, and both are joined to one another."[37]

(45) The A.D. 210 **Caius of Rome** was even more anti-chiliastic. He said[38] that the Gnostic heretic "Cerinthus, through 'revelations' he would have us believe were written by a great Apostle, brings before us 'marvellous things' which he pretends were shown him by Angels; alleging that **after** the resurrection...the flesh dwells in Jerusalem.... And, being an enemy to the Scripture of God - wishing to deceive men, he says there is to be a space of a thousand years for marriage festivals!"

(46) Was **Tertullian** a premillennialistic Chiliast - or a Historic **Postmillennialist**? Probably, he was a rare mixture of both! At times, he speaks of eternity as following **immediately** after the **resurrection**.[39] Even his *Against Marcion*, while indeed teaching the resurrection of the just "sooner or later" and "within" the thousand years,[40] nevertheless says nothing about the resurrection of the unjust unto damnation at the end of the thousand years. All of this is, of course, quite reconcilable with **non**-chiliastic views. Indeed, Tertullian's *Apology*[41] seems to indicate he believed Jesus was coming to judge all people **simultaneously**. Also Tertullian's frequently-quoted work called *Shows*,[42] does not establish that he was chiliastic.

(47) "**After** the casting of the Devil into the bottomless pit for a while [Revelation 20:2]" - explains Tertullian - "the blessed prerogative of the **first** resurrection may be ordained from the thrones [Revelation 20:4-6].... Then again, **after** the consignment of him to the fire [Revelation 20:10]..., the judgment of the **final** and **universal resurrection** may be determined out of the books [Revelation 20:12-14]."

(48) Yet perhaps his work *On the Resurrection of the Flesh*,[43] taken in conjunction with his *Antidote for the Scorpion's Sting*,[44] does imply **some** or other unique kind of 'Chiliasm.' However, even that is not **absolutely** clear. For it does not unimpeachably teach that the **first** resurrection is **physical**.

(49) In chapter 25 of his *Resurrection of the Flesh*, Tertullian seems to reject Chiliasm. He says: "The very maintenance of this **spiritual** resurrection, amounts to a presumption in favour of the other **bodily** resurrection. For if none were announced for that time – there would be fair ground for asserting **only** this 'purely **spiritual** resurrection.' Inasmuch, however, as (a resurrection) **is** proclaimed for the **last** time - it is proved to be a **bodily** one, because there is **no spiritual** one also **then** announced. For why make a **second** announcement of a resurrection of only one character - that is, the **spiritual** one – since this ought to be undergoing accomplishment either **now**, without any regard to different times, or else **then** at the very conclusion of all the periods? It is therefore more competent for us even to maintain a **spiritual** resurrection at the **commencement** of a **life of faith** – we who acknowledge the **full completion** thereof at the **end** of the World."

(50) Furthermore, Tertullian rejected[45] the 'any moment return' of Christ to this Earth – of all Dispensationalists and of most Premillennialists. For he denied that Christ would come again, **until** after the Pagan Roman State had first fallen away. The latter would only start occurring fully a century after his death, at its nominal christianization in A.D. 321 and further at its yet-later demise into ten kingdoms (in about A.D. 500f) after the A.D. 476 overthrow of the Western Roman Empire by the Barbarians. For only then would Antichrist (*cf.* the Romish Papacy from A.D. 606 onward) start to be introduced upon the ruins of the Roman Empire.

(51) On Tertullian's anti-dispensationalistic **eschatological optimism** regarding the **successful** course of the Gospel in our **present** World here and now, he says:[46] "'**All** kings shall fall down before Him.... **All nations** shall serve Him.' To Whom shall **all** thus do homage, but Christ? ... In Solomon was **no** nation blessed; in Christ, **every** nation!" Tertullian also writes:[47] "The Lord sent the Paraclete...so that...**discipline** should, **little by little**, be...carried on to **perfection**.... What then is the Paraclete's administrative office but this: the **direction** of discipline; the **revelation** of the Scriptures; the **reformation** of the intellect; the **advancement** toward the '**better** things'?"

(52) The A.D. 230 **Origen** was clearly **postmillennialistic**. Wrote he:[48] "Thus says Holy Scripture: 'The Lord said to My Lord, "Keep on sitting at My right hand, until I make Your enemies Your footstool!"' [Psalm 110:1].... 'For Christ must keep on reigning until He has put all enemies under His feet [First Corinthians 15:25].... 'For **all** things must be put **under** Him' [First Corinthians 15:27f].... The Lord Himself in the Gospel...declares that these same results are **future**.... They are to be brought about by His own **intercession**" - and **not** by His final visible ***Parousia***! "Thus the divine likeness itself already appears to **advance**" - toward its eschatological goal.

(53) Origen further stated in his *Against Celsus*: "It is evident that even the Barbarians, when they yield obedience to the Word of God, will become most obedient to the Law.... Every form of worship will be destroyed except the Christian Religion, which alone will prevail. And indeed it will one day triumph - as its principles take possession of the minds of men more and more every day."

(54) It is sometimes claimed that Cyprian and Methodius were Chiliasts. Such claims are not true! The A.D. 258 **Cyprian** was not a Premillennialist. For he clearly believed that Christ's **next** Coming would immediately be followed by the **Final Judgment**.[49] Nor was the A.D. 300 **Methodius** a Chiliast. For he too believed that the resurrection would immediately be followed by Judgment Day - and then by the eternal state.[50]

(55) Wrote Cyprian[51] (**during a time of great persecution**): "Let us be **armed**, beloved brethren, with our **whole** strength! And let us be prepared for the struggle with an uncorrupted mind; with a sound faith; with a devoted courage! Let the camp of God **go forth** to the **battlefield** which has been appointed to us! Let the **sound** ones be **armed** - lest he who **is** sound, should **lose** the **advantage** of having stood lately! Let the lapsed also be armed - so that even the **lapsed** may **regain** what he has lost...; taking the shield of faith, with which you shall be **able to quench** all the fiery darts of the wicked one.... **The Church**, which before had been barren, will have **more** children from among the **Gentiles**.... Christ our **God**...[is] the **Enlightener** and Saviour of the **human race**."

(56) It was **Victorinus** who, right **after the fiercest-ever persecution of Christians**, in A.D. 300 wrote the first extant commentary on the Book of Revelation. It is clearly **antichiliastic** - and **postmillennialistic**. Wrote Victorinus on Revelation 6:1-2: "The first seal being opened, he [the Apostle John] says he saw a white horse, and a crowned Horseman having a bow.... After the Lord ascended into Heaven and opened all things, He sent the Holy Spirit Whose words the Preachers sent forth like arrows, reaching to the human heart – so that they might **overcome unbelief**.... For [in Matthew 24:14] the Lord says: 'This Gospel shall be preached **throughout the whole World** for a testimony **to all nations**!'"[52]

(57) Victorinus further added on Revelation 20:1-5: "Those years in which Satan is bound, are at the **first** advent of Christ even **to** the **end** of the **age**. And they are called a **thousand**, according to that mode of speaking in which a part is signified by the whole - just as is that passage 'the Word which He commanded for a thousand generations' (although they are not a thousand).... He says that **he** [Satan] is bound and shut up so that he **may not keep on seducing the nations**. 'The **nations**' signifies the **Church** - seeing that **it** is itself **being formed** from **them**.... The '**first resurrection**' is **now**, of the **souls** that are by the Faith which does not permit men to pass over to 'the second death.' Of **this** resurrection, the Apostle says: 'If you **have** risen with Christ - **keep on** seeking those things which are above!'"[53]

(58) After the A.D. 313 accession of **Constantine** as the first Christian Emperor in Rome, the previously-persecuted Church was greatly advantaged. Exulted **Eusebius** around 321f: "Especially we who placed our hopes in the Christ of God, had unspeakable gladness.... A certain inspired joy bloomed for all of us - when **we** saw **every** place (which shortly before had been desolated by the impieties of the tyrants) **reviving** as if from a long and deathfraught pestilence, and **temples again rising** from their foundations to an **immense** height and receiving a splendour far **greater** than the old ones which had been destroyed.... 'For the Lord remembered us in our low estate, and **delivered** us from our adversaries!' (Psalm 136:23f)."[54]

(59) None of the above Early Church Fathers - from the A.D. 66f Apostles John and Barnabas, down to the A.D. 321f Eusebius - would feel at home among modern Pretribulationists (of whatever variety). After the **nominal christianization of the Roman Empire** by the first Christian Emperor Constantine in A.D. 321f - even the antipretribulationist kind of 'Christian Chiliasm' of Justin, Irenaeus and Tertullian died out for more than twelve centuries. It was hardly ever heard of again - until revived not by the Lutheran and Calvinistic Protestants but instead by the Non-Protestant Dutch Anabaptists.[55]

(60) From the time of John's Revelation in A.D. 66f down to the time of Justin Martyr almost a century later, there is **no trace of Chiliasm** in any of the extant writings of Christian Scholars. Though "Christian Chiliasm" did have a few genuinely-Christian advocates between the times of Justin Martyr in A.D. 150 and Lactantius in A.D. 310, it had **none whatsoever** in the many centuries since Constantine until almost the end of the Late Middle Ages.

(61) So-called 'Amillennialism' - is really postmillennial. For it too rightly says Christ will return visibly to resurrect all people simultaneously unto Final Judgment - only at the **end** of the millennium (however conceived). Even if modern 'Amillennialists' do not wish to be called Postmillennialists - all of them and also Premillennialists too need to know that **each and every Early Church Father before the A.D. 150 Justin Martyr - was a nonchiliastic Postmillennialist** (whether a **consistent optimist**, or whether **somewhat less hopeful**). So too was every Church Father from A.D. 230 until A.D. 300 - from Origen of Caesarea to Victorinus of Pettau.

(62) So too was each and every Early Church Father from the A.D. 321f Eusebius onward - such as Athanasius, Ephraim, Basil, Hilary, Cyril, Gregory of Nyssa, Gregory Nazianzen, Ambrose, Chrysostom, Jerome, Augustine, Vincent of Lerinum, and Gregory the Great. So too were Bede of Yarrow, Alcuin of York, Bruno of Segni, Anselm of Canterbury, Joachim of Floris, Thomas Aquinas, Roger Bacon, Pierre d'Olivi, Ubertino of Casale, John Wycliffe, Matthias of Janow, Nicholas de Cusa, Savanarola, and Christopher Columbus. So too were **all** of the Protestant Reformers - including Luther and Calvin.[56]

(63) Rev. Prof. Dr. Martin Luther wrote:[57] "In the beginning, the Church was **victorious** over...the Jews and the might of the Romans. In like manner, she will **today** and **forever** be **victorious**...over the Pope and the power of the Turk.... The Pope is the last blaze in the lamp which will go out, and ere long be extinguished.... But when he is struck with God's Word - then the Pope is turned to a poppy and a frothy flower!"

(64) In his *Institutes* III:25:5, Rev. Prof. Dr. John Calvin rejects the '**heavenly** millennium' theory (held also by

many modern 'Amillennialists') - as well as the views of "the Chiliasts" or the Premillennialists "who **limited** the **reign** of Christ to a thousand years.... Those who assign **only** a thousand years to the children of God to enjoy... observe not how great an insult they offer to Christ and His Kingdom.... If their blessedness is to have an end, the Kingdom of Christ...is temporary. In short, they are either most ignorant of all divine things - or they maliciously aim at subverting the whole grace of God and power of Christ which cannot have their **full** effect unless sin is obliterated, death swallowed up, and **eternal** life **fully** renewed."

(65) This chiliastic "**fiction**" and "**dream**" (says Calvin), is "too **puerile** to need or to deserve refutation." Nor do they "receive any countenance from the Apocalypse (*viz.* Revelation 20:4), from which it is known that they extracted a gloss for their error – since the thousand years **there** mentioned, refer **not to the eternal blessedness of the Church**, but only to" those events "which **await** the Church Militant **in this World**" (and thus here on **Earth**).

(66) In his *Psychopannychia*, Calvin adds: "John has described a twofold resurrection...; namely one [resurrection] of the **soul**, **before** judgment - and another when **the body will be raised up** and when the soul also will be raised up to glory. 'Blessed,' says he, 'are those who have part in the first resurrection; on them the second death takes **no effect**' (Revelation 20:6).... That **first resurrection**...is the only **entrance** - to **beatific glory**."

(67) Calvin wrote too:[58] "Salvation to the **whole World** was to **proceed**.... The glory...will diffuse its splendour **far and wide**.... God Himself will cause the beams of His grace to shine into **distant lands** - so that **kings**

and nations may be united - into fellowship with the children of Abraham.... It would be extended - **to the uttermost boundaries of the Earth**..., so as to occupy **the whole World**."

(68) Calvin continues:[59] "The whole World **will be brought into subjection to the authority of Christ**.... The nations **will be convinced** that nothing is more desirable than to receive from Him Laws and Ordinances.... David therefore with good reason prays that the glory of the Divine Name may **fill the whole Earth** - since **that Kingdom was to be extended even to the uttermost boundaries of the Globe**."

(69) The genius of Geneva further insists:[60] "Our doctrine must stand sublime above all the glory of the World, and **invincible** by all its power. Because it is not ours, but that of the Living God and His Anointed Whom the Father has appointed King so that He may **rule from Sea to Sea** and from the rivers **even to the ends of the Earth** - and so rule, as to **smite the whole Earth**...with the mere **Rod of His Mouth** and break them into pieces like a potter's vessel according to the magnificent predictions of the Prophets respecting His Kingdom. Daniel 2:34; Isaiah 11:4; Psalm 2:9."

(70) Calvin's Student John Knox taught the same in Scotland: "Perceiving how Satan in his members, the Antichrist of our time, cruelly rages seeking to downthring and to destroy the Evangel of Christ and His Congregation, **we ought** according to our bounden duty to strive in our Master's cause even unto death - being **certain** of the **victory** in **Him**.... Arise, O Lord, and let Thine enemies be confounded! Let them who hate Thy godly Name flee from Thy presence! Give Thy servants strength to speak Thy Word with boldness! And **let all nations cleave to the true knowledge of Thee!**"[61]

(71) John Knox and Mrs. John Calvin's brother-in-law William Whittingham wrote the Calvinistic *Geneva Bible*. That declares:[62] "Christ [is the Stone] Who was sent by God...Whose Kingdom at the beginning would be small" - but which "would **at length grow** and **fill the whole Earth**.... The **Jews...and the Gentiles** - shall **embrace Christ**.... The **World shall be restored** to a new life.... The time shall come that **the whole nation of the Jews**, though not every one particularly, **shall be joined to the Church of Christ**."

(72) The *Heidelberg Catechism* of Olevianus and Ursinus proclaims:[63] "**Thy Kingdom come**! That is, so govern us by Thy Word and Spirit - so that we may **submit** ourselves **more and more** to Thee! Preserve and **increase** Thy **Church**! **Destroy the works of the Devil** and all power that would exalt itself against Thee and also all wicked counsels devised against Thy Holy Word - till the full perfection of Thy Kingdom shall have come! ... Do Thou therefore preserve and **strengthen** us by the power of Thy Holy Spirit, so that we may...not sink in this spiritual warfare but constantly and **strenuously resist** our foes till at last **we obtain a complete victory**!"

(73) The *Belgic Confession* of Guido de Bres declares:[64] "**We still use the testimonies taken out of the Law** and the Prophets, to confirm us in the doctrine of the Gospel, and to regulate our life in all honesty to the glory of God according to His will.... We believe that our gracious God...**will that the World should be governed by certain Laws**.... For this purpose, **He has committed the sword to the Magistrate**.... Their office is...that they protect the sacred Ministry, and thus may **remove and prevent all idolatry** and false-worship, so that the kingdom of **Antichrist may be destroyed** and the **Kingdom of Christ promoted**."

(74) This same postmillennial perspective was promoted also by Theodore Beza, William Perkins, Richard Hakluyt, John Foxe, James the First, Thomas Brightman, J.H. Alsted, Richard Sibbes, Gijsbert Voetius, Samuel Rutherford, John Cotton, William Twisse, and the Westminster Assembly of 1643f. Thus the *Westminster Larger Catechism* of British Calvinists states that "Christ executeth the office of a King in calling...a people...and giving them...**Laws**...by which He visibly governs them...and [in] **overcoming all their enemies**." In the Lord's Prayer the phrase 'The Kingdom come!' is a petition "that the kingdom of sin and **Satan may be destroyed**, the Gospel propagated throughout the World, the **Jews called**, the **fullness of the Gentiles brought in**" - and that **the Church** be "furnished with all Gospel- Officers and ordinances; **purged from corruption**; [and be] countenanced and **maintained by the Civil Magistrate**."[65]

(75) The *Westminster Confession of Faith*, which states[66] that God "hath ordained the **Civil Magistrates** to be under Him...for His Own glory and the publick good...[and] hath armed them with the power of the sword for the defence and **encouragement of those that are good** and for the **punishment of evil-doers**." It was expanded even further in the *Savoy Declaration* of 1658. That says:[67] "There is no other Head of the Church but the Lord Jesus Christ.... The Pope of Rome...is that **Antichrist...whom the Lord shall destroy**.... In the **latter days** - Antichrist being **destroyed**, the **Jews called** and the **adversaries** of the Kingdom of His dear Son **broken** - the **churches** of Christ, being **enlarged** and edified through a free and plentiful communication of light and grace, shall enjoy in

this World a **more** quiet...and **glorious condition** than they have enjoyed" till now.

(76) Also after the Westminster Assembly, the postmillennial perspective has been championed by a great cloud of witnesses almost too great even to number. Of such, we here mention only: Owen, Eliot, Van Riebeeck, Dickson, Charnock, Greenhill, Samuel Lee, Brooks, John Brown of Wamphray, Essenius, Spener, Bunyan, Cocceius, Newton, Howe, Cameron, Durham, Witsius, the Mathers, Koelman, Baxter, Vitringa, Matthew Henry, Brakel, Boston, Lampe, Fleming, Willison, Lowman, Edwards, Whitefield, Bengel, the Wesleys, Doddridge, Gill, John Brown of Haddington, Flavel, Dwight, Fuller, Carey, Hopkins, Clarke, Haldane, Neander, Faber, Livingstone, Alexander, David Brown, Hengstenberg, Paton, Barnes, Thornwell, Fairbairn, Spurgeon, the Hodges, Martensen, Dabney, Andrew Murray, Trench, Dorner, John Kennedy, Shedd, Symington, Candlish, Meyer, Girardeau, Schaff, Strong, Warfield, MacFarlane, Snowden, Machen, Schilder, Zwemer, Carroll, Craig, Boettner, Gerstner, John Murray, Kik, R.B. Kuiper, Latourette, Van Til, and Rushdoony.[68]

(77) We summarize. **None** of the books of the Bible **nor** any extant writings of the Earliest Church Fathers - such as the *Didachee* or *Teaching of the Twelve Apostles* (A.D. 97), the *Epistle of Barnabas* (98), Clement of Rome (98), Hermas (100), Ignatius (107), Quadratus (120), the *Epistle to Diognetus* (130), Pseudo-Clement (135), Polycarp (140), or Papias (145) - are chiliastic. With the exception of the Mid-Patristic Justin (150), Irenaeus (185), Tertullian (200) and those who followed them - none of the later Patristic Fathers were Chiliasts.

(78) In fact, **all** mainline Ante-Nicene Fathers even after Justin - **in spite of living during times when the Church was often persecuted by the Pagan Roman Empire** - strongly opposed Chiliasm and all other forms of Escapism. Thus Tatian (A.D. 155), Theophilus (170), Melito (173), Claudius Apollinarius (175), Hegesippus (178),[69] Athenagoras (185), Clement of Alexandria (190), Caius (210), Hippolytus (220), Origen (230), Dionysius of Alexandria (255), Cyprian (258), Methodius (290), Victorinus (300), and the writers of the 310 *Apostolic Constitutions*.[70]

(79) Even throughout **that** period, the vast majority of Christian Leaders maintained their eschatological **optimism**. Indeed, the only reason why **even then** (and indeed only from the middle of the second century onward) just a **minority** of Christians adopted any form of Chiliasm at all - would seem to be because of the eschatological pessimism which plagued that minority in their sufferings under the Pagan-Roman persecutions from 150 until 313 A.D.

(80) After the triumph of Christianity at the nominal christianization of Pagan Rome (in A.D. 313-321), the chiliastic "double resurrections" theory was phased out of Christianity altogether - for more than a thousand years. During the subsequent Post-Constantinian centuries of victorious Christianity, there are no traces of Chiliasm. It is totally absent from all of the many writings of Eusebius (A.D. 330), Athanasius (340), Aphrahat (350), Ephraim (360), Hilary (365), Basil (370), Cyril (375), Gregory of Nyssa (380), Gregory Nazianzen (385), Ambrose (390), Chrysostom (400), Sulpicius Severus (410), Jerome (415), and the mature Augustine of Hippo-Regius (420).

(81) Furthermore, it is also totally absent in all of the (strongly optimistic) Post-Augustinian Theologians right down to the climax of Christian influence in the sixteenth century Protestant Reformation and in Puritanism in the middle of the seventeenth century. Both the Early Lutherans and the Early Calvinists condemned Premillennialism. Instead, the *Westminster Larger Catechism* (QQ. 191f) and the *Savoy Declaration* (26:4f) implicitly reassert the **Biblical Postmillennialism** of the Earliest Church Fathers.

(82) Only little groups like the Dutch Anabaptists and their successors kept the chiliastic theory alive on the very fringes of Christianity during those centuries after the Protestant Reformation. Indeed, prior to the advent of that **great** opponent of Christian Civilization - the 1789 French Revolution (and her subsequent daughters of Humanism and Socialism) - Chiliasm was all but unknown. Not until Europe in the 1830s, did Revolutionary Pretribulationism ever develop. And it is only **since** then that **the modern revolutionary trend** - with its ungodly opposition to and persecution of the truth - has turned some Christians (by way of frustration) **away from victory** in this present age, **and toward rapturistic defeatism**.

(83) It is necessary for Christians to overcome the alien revolutionary spirit now prevalent in our modern World! The People of God today must conquer the pessimistic spirit of *Quasi*-Christian defeatism which modern **Anti**-Christian Revolutionists would so gladly encourage among Christians.

(84) The Church of the twenty-first century must recovery the optimistic spirit of a **victorious** Christianity - that of Jesus' first-century Apostles; of His second-century Apostolic Fathers; of His third-century Martyrs;

of His fourth-century Conquerors; of His mediaeval *Corpus Christianum* Theologians; of His sixteenth-century Protestant Reformers; and of His seventeenth-century Puritans. The Church of the twenty-first century must ditch Premillennialism and instead become a Church of **Overcomers**. For there is absolutely no substitute - for **Christian Victory**.

(85) So then, in the words of John's Revelation (15:4 & 20:6 & 21:24-26): "Who shall **not** fear You, O Lord, and glorify Your Name? For You alone are holy. For **all nations shall come and worship before You**.... They shall be priests of God and of Christ, and shall reign with Him **a thousand years**.... The **nations**[71] **shall walk in the light** [of the Holy City].... **The kings of the Earth...shall bring** the glory and **honour of the nations into it**!"

THE END

ENDNOTES

1 J. Walvoord's *The Millennial Kingdom*, Zondervan, Grand Rapids, 1959, pp. 120ff; *per contra* G.E. Ladd's *The Blessed Hope*, Eerdmans, Grand Rapids, 1956, p. 31. D. MacPherson's cited books were all published by Heart of America Bible Society, Kansas City, Mo.

2 *Cf.* F.C. Fensham's *The Messiah is Coming!*, D.R.C. Booksellers, Cape Town, 1957. See too: Gen. 1:26-28; 2:1-3; 3:15; 9:1-16; 12:1-4; 17:4-8; 18:18f; 22:15-18; 26:1-4 & v. 26; 28:1-6,20f; 49:9f; Lev. chs. 23 to 25; Num. 14:21; Judg. 4:13 & v. 31; Pss. 2 & 22 & 72 & 110.

3 Joel 2:28-32; Am. 9:11-15; Isa. 2:2-20; 9:6f; 11:6-10; 49:22f; 60:2-5; 66:12-23; Mic. 4:1-5; 5:2-4; Zeph. 2:11f; 3:9f; Hab. 2:14,20; Jer. 3:16f; 23:5f; 31:31-34; Ob. 15-21; Ezek. 47:8-12; Dan. 2:34f,44; 7:13f,27; Zech. 2:4f,11; 9:9f; 14:9-16; Mal. 1:11 *etc.*

4 Ex. 3:6; Mt. 22:29-32; Job. 19:25-27; Isa. 26:19; Ezek. 37:1-14; Dan. 12:2.

5 Eccl. 12:1-14; Dan. 12:2f; Mal. chs. 3 & 4.

6 According to the *Old Testament Pseudepigrapha*, the Messianic period was to commence in 5000 *A.M.* (= *Anno Mundi* alias 'after the creation of the World'). Thus *Assumpt. Moses* 1:1 & 10:29. Or in 6000 *A.M.* (thus *I Enoch* chs. 91 to 104 & *II Enoch* 33:1 & *II Baruch* 67). Or after "twelve parts" each of perhaps 500 years' duration (thus *IV Ezra* 14:11 & *II Baruch* 53f) - and not long after the +/- B.C. 107 writing down of the *Book of Jubilees* (*Jub.* Chs. 15 & 23:30f). See too *I Enoch* and *Test. 12 Pat.* with P.A. Verhoef's *Messianic Expectation Between the Old and New Testament* (D.R.C. Pub., Cape Town, 1959).

7 The *Book of Jubilees* says that the 'Golden Age' would gradually be realized by an ethical and physical transformation of the Earth during a 1000-year period, until international bliss and spiritual immortality was reached (*I Baruch* 5:1-7; *Syb. Orac.* III:46-50; *I Enoch* 10:21f; *Test. Levi* 4:3f & 18:2-12; *Test. Judah* 22:2; *Test. Zeb.* 9:8; *Test. Asher* 7:3; *Test. Joseph* 19:11f;

Jub. chs. 1 & 15 & 23:26-30f; *DSS* in *Bened.* 1 Q 5b III:25,28). It was believed that this period would last: for 400 years (thus *II Esdras* 7:28f); for 1000 years (thus *II Enoch* 33:1 & *Jub.* 23:26-29); temporarily, for three "World-weeks" (thus *I Enoch* 91:12-19 & chs. 93 to 104); or permanently (thus *I Enoch* chs. 1 to 5 & 11:2 & 83 to 90).

8 *Jub.* chs. 15 & 23:29 and *Test. Levi* 18:12.

9 *I Enoch* chs. 37 to 70 (esp. 51:1f & 61:5-8b & 91:9-11 & 100:5); *Test. Benj.* 10:18; *II Baruch* 30:1-5; *Syb. Orac.* IV:187-91. Ancient Samaritan theology too knows of only one resurrection (*cf.* M. Gaster's *Samaritan Eschatology*, pp. 114-18). Also the Post-Christian Judaistic *Talmud* (developing the previous ideas) knows nothing of the chiliastic doctrine of chronologically-separated physical resurrections. *Cf.* W. Masselink's *Millennial Kingdom*,

Meinema, Delft, 1932, pp. 30f.

10 *Test. Judah* 25:1,4; *II Esdras* 7:28-35; *II Macc.* 7:9-11,14,23 & 12:44 & 14:46; *I Enoch* chs. 37 to 71 & 91:10 & chs. 91 to 104 & esp. 100:5.

11 Mt. chs. 1 to 5; Lk. chs. 1 to 4; Rev. chs. 1 & 5 to 9 & 20:1-7.

12 Acts ch. 2; Col. 1:13-20; Rev. 1:5,18; 20:1f; 22:16.

13 I Cor. 15:24-28 *cf.* Mt. 24:14; 28:18-20; Acts 1:5-8; Rev. 1:5-9; 12:11; 17:14; 20:1-6.

14 Jh. 5:28f; Acts 24:15; I Cor. 15:23; Phil. 3:20f; I Th. 4:16; Rev. 20:13-15.

15 Mt. 25:31-46; Jh. 5:27-29; 6:39f,44,54; 11:24; Rev. 20:7-15.

16 John's Rev. 20:4-6 *cf.* 3:1. *Cf.* the same John in his Gospel 3:15-18 & 5:21-29 esp. vv. 24F & 6:40,47 & 8:51 & 11:25 & 20:31; and the same John in his Epistle I Jh. 3:14 & 5:13. See too: Rom. 6:3-13; 7:4-9; 8:6-13; 11:15; Eph. 2:1-6; 5:14; Gal. 2:20; Phil. 1:21; Col. 2:12f; 3:1-3 & I Pet. 1:3. See too M. Kline's *First Resurrection* (in *Westm. Theol. Journ.*, Westminster Theol. Sem., Philadelphia, Spring 1975). There, Kline -

reminiscent of Tertullian's *On the Resurrection of the Flesh* ch. 25, as cited in nn. 43 & 46 below (*q.v.*), points out that the "first resurrection" guarantees escape from the second death, Rev. 20:5b- 6a, thus suggesting spiritual resurrection or regeneration (Jh. 3:3-8). Kline also points out that it is a "first resurrection" rather than a 'new resurrection' - thus implying an event within time, and not at the end of it. *Cf.* the similar use of the word "first" [within time] in Heb. 8:7,13 & 9:1,18 & 10:9. See too (in Rev. 21:1,1,5) the use of the word "new" at the end of time.

17 *Cf.* John's Rev. 20:5ab,7f. See too Ezek. chs. 38 & 38 (esp. vv. 3,8f,12,14). Also *cf.* John's Rev. 20:12-15 & 21:7f & 22:11f,17-20 with the same John's Gospel, and with Mt. As mentioned in n. 15 above.

18 Rev. 20:3-7,10-15; 21:1,17; 22:1 & *cf.* nn. 5 & 14 & 15 above.

19 Masselink's *op. cit.* pp. 30f *cf.* Tiele's *Religion of Zarathustra*, Kruseman, Haarlem, 1864, pp. 250f & esp. 254. In the B.C. 1000 to B.C. 500f Zoroastrian eschatology, the serpent Azi-Dahak is bound inside Mt. Damavend for 9000 years. It breaks its bonds in the last days - but only speedily then to be conquered for all time by the Fredun, who then awakens from his slumbers. See *Yast.* III:52-60 & *Bundahesh* 29:8. See too Noss's *Man's Religions*, New York, Macmillan, 1967, pp. 487 & 556f. *Cf.* too ed. J.D. Douglas's *New International Dictionary of the Christian Church*, Zondervan, Grand Rapids, 1974, pp. 294,625,1072.

20 *Cf.* Irenaeus's *Against Heresies* V:30-36 with Justin Martyr's *Dialogue with Trypho* (81f), and the partial absorption (by Tertullian in the Phrygian colony of Carthage) of Montanistic Chiliasm from Phrygia in Asia Minor. See D.H. Kromminga's book *The Millennium in the Church*, Eerdmans, Grand Rapids, 1945, pp. 77f. This Phrygian theatre of Neo-Chiliasm, is significant. For Phrygia in Asia seems to have been the central dissemination point of this 2nd to 3rd century A.D. brand of Chiliasm on the fringes of Christianity. The heretic Cerinthus (A.D. 100f), who was also a Chiliast, hailed from Phrygia. See Douglas's *op. Cit.* p. 207. Papias (A.D. 145) and Justin Martyr (A.D. 150) both seem to have been in contact with that region. And so too do Irenaeus (A.D. 185) and the A.D. 220 Tertullian (thus Kromminga's *op. cit.* pp 29 & 44 & 53 & 77 & 89). No doubt Cerinthus picked up the "Phrygian heresy" of Chiliasm from those more-eastern Asian quarters of Persia and Babylon. Even Augustine (*City of God* 20:7) - himself chiliastic during the earlier period of his Manichaean and Post-Manichaean life - prior to his conversion to Christ(ianity) - appears to have derived that Chiliasm from Persian Manichaeism (*cf.* n. 19 above). See too Van der Leeuw & Bleeker's volumes *The Religions of the World*, Meulenhoff, Amsterdam, 1956, II:136. Moreover, it should be noted that the Chiliast Justin Martyr was also rationalistic and subordinationistic. The Chiliast Irenaeus upheld other doctrinal errors too - holding to baptismal regenerationism, episcopalianism, and believing that Lot's wife continued menstruating even after being turned into a pillar of salt. Even the offbeat suspected Chiliast Tertullian was both legalistic and Semi-Montanistic. Modern Premillennialists who appeal to the assumed 'Chiliasm' of Justin and Irenaeus and Tertullian - assuming them to be orthodox in all their theology (so that their Chiliasm too should then also be deemed to be orthodox) - should therefore be evaluated with caution if not also with scepticism.

21 *Cf.* nn. 2 & 3 above and: Pss. 72 & 89; Isa. chs. 40 to 66; Ezek. chs. 40f; Am. ch. 9; Mic. ch. 4; Hab. ch. 2; Hag. ch. 2; Zech. chs. 6 & 9 & 14; Mal. chs. 3 & 4; *etc*. Moreover, the apocryphal I Macc. 14:8-10 alleges the partial realization of this 'Golden Age' in about 100 B.C.

22 *E.g.* ancient heathen accounts - such as the *Merneptah Legend* in Egypt; the Babylonian *Codex Hammurabi*; the Assyrian prosperity of Assurbanipal; the Zoroastrian 'Golden Age'; the Elysian fields of Greek mythology; Virgil's Pagan-Roman 'millennium'; Stoic and Epicurean futurologies; the 'Cargo' religions of the South Pacific; and even modern Humanism's idyllic or mechanized Utopias. All of these, of course, are to some extent based upon (and perversions of) God's original and ongoing revelations of the Paradise tradition with its promise of a future 'Paradise Regained.' *Cf.*: Gen. chs. 1 & 2 and esp. 2:1-3 with Heb. 4:9-11; Gen. 2:15-17 & 3:17-22 *cf.* Rev. 2:7 & 22:2; Gen. 3:15 *cf.* Acts 14:11; Gen. 5:29 *cf.* Rev. 14:13; Gen. 9:9-16 & 11:1-9; Isa. chs. 11 & 65 & 66; Acts 14:15-17; 17:22-34; Rev. 20:1-6; *etc.* See too Breasted's *Ancient Records of Egypt*, III:263; Harper's *Code of Hammurabi*, pp. 3f; Harper's *Assyrian and Babylonian Letters*, I:2:2f; Carnoy's *Mythology of All Races* VI:304 (citing *Yasna* IX:4f) & VI:308 (citing *Vendidad* II:27f); Hesiod's *Theogony* and *Works and Days*; Plutarch's *Sartorius* 8f; Horace's *Epodes* 16; Virgil's *Eclogues* (IV:9:46) & *Georgics* (I:121f) & *Aeneid* (VI:788f); Seneca's *Natural Questions* (III:30:7); and Vanderwaal's *The Revelation of Jesus Christ*, De Vuurbaak, Groningen, 1971, pp. 130f.

23 *Cf.* Gen. chs. 1 to 11; Acts chs. 14 & 17; Rom. chs. 1 & 2. *Cf.* too Job 32:8 & Gen. 6:1-3.

24 Thus L. Berkhof's *History of Christian Doctrine*, Eerdmans, Grand Rapids, 1959, p. 270.

Cf. Kromminga's *op. cit.* pp. 77f with Irenaeus's *op. cit.* (I:26:1 & III:3:4 & III:11:1); Caius's *Fragments* I:2; Tertullian's *On Modesty*, his *On Fasting*, and his *On Monogamy*; Dionysius Alexandrinus's *Fragments* I:3; Hippolytus's *Refutation of All Heresies* (VV:21 & X:17); Eusebius's *Church History* (III:28:1f & VII:25:1-3); and Augustine's *On Heresy* (I:8).

25 Justin Martyr's *Dialogue with Trypho*, chs. 80f. Note that the Samaritan Justin's "Chiliasm"

- derived from the East (II Kgs. 17:24ff) - was chiefly motivated only by his desire to 'christianize' the 'chiliazed' Jew Trypho. Unlike our modern Chiliasts, Justin believed that Christ would give the 'Holy Land' to all Christians (be they converts from the Judaists or from the Gentiles). And he also believed that they would reside there for an eternal or never-ending "thousand years"; during which "time" believers would be immortal(-ized) permanently. See his *Dial.* ch. 45 *cf.* chs. 39, 113, 121, 132 & 139.

26 John the Baptizer, Jesus, the Apostles, the Apostolic Fathers, and the Earliest Apologists all seem to have been Postmillennialists. See: Lk. 1:76-79; Jh. 12:31; Mt. 28:18-20; Acts 2:38f; II Pet. 3:8f; I Cor. 15:22-28; Col. 1:17-20; Jh. 1:1-14; I Jh. 3:8 & 4:1,4,14 & 5:4; Rev. 11:15 & 12:10 & 14:12 & 15:3f & 20:1-6 & 21:23-26; *Did.* 9:4 & 10:5 & 14:3; *Barn.* 6:12-19 & ch. 12; *I Clem* chs. 33 & 36f; *Hermas* I:3:4,8 & I:4:2; Ignatius's *Epistles to the Magnesians* (1:13f & 2:10-14) and *To Polycarp* (ch. 3); *Epistle to Diognetus*, chs. 5 & 7.

27 Thus even the Premillennialist Irenaeus (*op. cit.* V:33:4).

28 The *Epistle of Barnabas* (ch. 15), possibly under the influence of *Second Enoch* 32:2 to 33:1 - and certainly under the influence of Holy Scripture (Gen. 2:1-3 *cf.* Heb. 4:9-11 & Mal.4:3-5) - specifically advocates the future advent of a Golden Age after the first coming of the Lord Jesus and toward the end of the World. Papias (*Fragment IV* in the Eerdmans ed. of the *Ante-Nicene Fathers* I:153*ff*) describes a future time of plentiful earthly activity reminiscent not only of that described in the (apparently postmillenial!) approx. B.C. 220 *Apoc. Baruch* 29:5 & chs. 50 & 51, the approx. 170f B.C. *Sybilline Oracles* III:744f, and the approx. B.C. 130 *Ethiopic Enoch* 10:19 (and also in the *Midrash on Genesis 27:28*) - but, more remotely, described from B.C. 800 onward also in the Older Testament itself (Am. 9:13f & Isa. 20:23-26). Note, however, that there are no extant writings of the A.D. 145 Papias himself. All we know about his teachings, is recorded in the writings of the A.D. 185 Premillennialist Irenaeus (*op. cit.* V:32 & V:33:3f & V:36) and in those of the A.D. 320 Postmillennialist Eusebius (*Ch. Hist.* III:39:8-12). Eusebius at III:36:2 n. 3 seems to have called Papias "a man most learned in all things"; but at III:39:13, a man "of very limited understanding" (*sic*!), when he obviously disapproves of what he regards as Papias's crass materialism and when Eusebius alleges Papias "says that there will be a millennium after the resurrection from the dead, when the personal reign of Christ will be established on this Earth." Yet Eusebius does not teach that Papias was a Chiliast who believed in two resurrections widely separated from one another. Indeed, Papias's *Fragment I* (from Euseb.: *Ch. Hist. III:39*) is truly Antiantinomian; and *Fragment V* (from Iren.: *Her.* V:36), citing I Cor. 15:25-28), is perhaps even postmillennial!

29 Iren.: *op. cit.* V:33:4.

30 See our text at nn. 39 to 47 below.

31 Just. Mart.: *Dial. with Trypho*, chs. 109-10.

32 Tatian's *To the Greeks* (VI).

33 Athenag.: *Plea for the Christians* ch. 31; and his *The Resurrection of the Dead* chs. 14,18,23 & 25.

34 *Op. cit.*, V:33:4f.

35 *Op. cit.*, V:13:1 & V:24:2 & V:35:1.

36 Iren.: *Fragments from the Lost Writings of Irenaeus* (XII), in *The Ante-Nicene Fathers*, Eerdmans, Grand Rapids, 1969 ed., I:570 & at its n. 2.

37 Clem. Alex.: *Miscellanies* VI:18, and *Fragments from the Latin Translation of Cassiodorus* I:1 (in *Ante-Nic. Fathers*, II:571).

38 Caius: *Fragments* I:1f.

39 Tert.: *Monogamy* 143 and *Hermogenes* 11.

40 Tert.: *Against Marcion*, III:25. Tert. writes: "We do confess that a kingdom is promised to us upon the Earth although before Heaven, only in another state of existence – inasmuch as it will be after the resurrection for a thousand years.... After its thousand years are over, within which period is completed the resurrection of the saints who rise sooner or later...there will ensue the destruction of the World and the conflagration of all things at the judgment."

41 Tert.: *Apology* 23.

42 Tert.: *Shows* 30.

43 Tert.: *On the Resurrection of the Flesh* 25.

44 Tert.: *Antidote for the Scorpion's Sting* 12.

45 Tert.: *Resurrection* 24.

46 Tert.: *Ag. Marc.* V:10.

47 Tert.: *On the Veiling of Virgins* I.

48 Orig.: *On the Fundamentals*, I:6:1 & II:11:2f III:6:1; and *Against Celsus*, 8:68.

49 Cyprian's *Tost.* 28 I, 44f, 76 (see the Premillennialist Kromminga's *op. cit.* pp. 69-71).

50 Methodius's *On the Resurrection* (I:8) and his *Banquet of the Ten Virgins* (IX:3) and his *Symposium* (IX:1-3).

51 Cyp.: *Epistle* 55 (58):2,5,8 and *Treatise* XII: 1 Test. 20 & 2 Test. 7.

52 Victorinus: *Commentary on the Apocalypse*, 6:1f.

53 *Ib.*, 20:1f.

54 Euseb.: *Ch. Hist.,* X:2:1 to X:4:9.

55 *Viz.*: Hoffmann, Matthijs, Beukelssen, Joris, Nicholas, and Menno Simons. Thus Kromminga: *op. cit.*, pp. 170-77.

56 Eusebius's *Ch. Hist.* (X:2-4); Athanasius's *On the Incarnation of the Word of God* (40 & 55); Ephraim the Syrian's *Hymn on the Nativity* (XVIII:1,6); Basil's *On the Six Days* (V:7); Hilary's *Homilies on the Psalms* (I); Cyril's *Catechet. Lectures* 15:1-3); Gregory of Nyssa's *Epistles* (17); Gregory of Nazianze's *Orations* (7:24); Ambrose's *Duties of the Clergy*(I:28:132f), his *On the Christian Faith* (V:14:181), and his *Enarrations in the Psalms* (43:7); Chrysostom's *Fourth Homily on Second Thessalonians*; Jerome's *Epistles* (53) and his *Commentary on Daniel* (2:40); Augustine's *City of God* (18:47f & 20:9 & 22:1,24), his *Fourth Treatise on the Gospel of John* (4), and his *Against Faustus* (13:7). Post-Augustinian Postmillennialists would include: Vincent of Lerinum (*Common Places* 23:547); Gregory the Great (*Epistle* 53), Bede of Yarrow (*Explanation of the Apocalypse*, in J.P. Migne's *Patrologia Latina* XCIII col. 146f); Alcuin of York (*Commentary on the*

Apocalypse, in Migne's *op. cit.* C cols. 1085 & 1156); Bruno of Segni (*Expositions*, in Migne's *op. cit.* CLXV cols. 667f); Anselm of Canterbury (*Dialogues*, in Migne's *op. cit.* CLXXXVIII cols. 1149f); Joachim of Floris (*Exposition of the Apocalypse*, 1527 ed., fols. 210r. *cf.* 84v & 211v *cf.* 16r); Thomas Aquinas (*Exposition of Daniel* ch. 2 p. 15 & ch. 7 pp. 34-4 in *Opera Omnia* XVIII, and *Summa Theologiae* pp. 105-12 as referred to in Kromminga's *op. cit.* p. 151); Roger Bacon's *Compendium Eludii Philosophiae* (as cited in Kromminga's *op. cit.* p. 158); Pierre d'Olivi (*Postilla on the Apocalypse*, Paris, fol. 18 r. col. 1 line 32 to col. 2 line 15); Ubertino of Casale (*Arbor Vitae* V ch. 12 and his *Tract.* ch. 8 fol. 78 r. cited in Froom's *op. cit.* I pp. 775v & 780n.);, John Wycliffe (*Concerning the Truth of Holy Scripture*, Truebner, 1905f ed., III:267f), and his *Concerning the Power of the Pope* (ch. II); Matthias of Janow (as cited in A. Neander's *General History of the Christian Religion and Church* V:200); Nicholas de Cusa (*Opera Conjectura* pp. 933f); Savanarola (*Predica della Rinnovazione* III and his *Sermon of March 1498* as quoted in Doellinger's *Prophecies and the Prophetic Spirit in the Christian Era*, Rivington's, London, 1873, pp. 149 & 163), Christopher Columbus (as cited in Harris's *Notes on Columbus* pp. 139f and in Draper's *History of the Intellectual Development of Europe*, Harper & Row, New York, 1876, II:159f). See too: S.J. Case's *The Millennial Hope*, University Press, Chicago, 1918, p. 181; and Kromminga's *op. cit.* That all Augustinian and Post-Augustinian and Puritan Theologians were Anti-Pretribulationistic and even largely Postmillennialistic, is generally conceded even by most Premillennialists. See L.E. Froom's *The Prophetic Faith of Our Fathers*, Review & Herald, Washington D.C., I-IV, 1945f; Kromminga's *op. cit.*; J. Walvoord's *The Millennial Kingdom*, Dunham Pub. Co., Findlay Oh., 1959; and I.H. Murray's *The Puritan Hope: Revival and the Interpretation of Prophecy*, Banner of Truth, London.

57 M. Luther: *Writings*, Germany, XXII col. 844, and his *Table Talk* p. 194.

58 J. Calvin: *Commentary* on Ps. 47 (Preamble and on vv. 7f).

59 J. Calvin: *Commentary* on Ps. 72:11.

60 J. Calvin: *Preface to King Francis*, para. 10 (in Calvin's *Institutes of the Christian Religion*).

61 J. Knox: *History of the Reformation in Scotland* (in his *Works*, Edinburgh, 1846-64 Woodrow Society ed., I:273) and as cited in Ridley's *John Knox*, 1968, p. 327 and in the *Scots Confession* 25:2 (co-authored chiefly by Knox).

62 *Geneva Bible* on Dan. 2:45 and on Rom. 11:25f (Univ. of Wisconsin Press, Madison, 1969).

63 *Heidelberg Catechism*, Q. & A. 123 & 127.

64 *Belgic Confession of Faith*, chs. XXV & XXXVI.

65 *Westminster Larger Catechism*, QQ. 45 & 191f.

66 *Westminster Confession of Faith*, 23:1.

67 *Savoy Declaration*, 26:4f.

68 For particulars, see F.N. Lee: *Christocratic Postmillennialism, 4000 B.C. to 2000 A.D.*, Wavell Hgts, Australia, unpub., 1999.

69 See Eusebius's *Ch. Hist.* IV:22-27 & V:14-29 & VI:20:3 (& *cf.* III:28 & VII:24).

70 *Pseudo-Clem*. 20:4; Mel.: *PP* 102; Claudius Apollin. (in Euseb. *Pref. Chron. Pasc.*); Iren.: *Ag. Her.* III:18:6 & III:23:1.7 & V:21:3; Hippol.: *LD* IV:33:4-5; *Apost. Const.*, VII:25f.

71 Erasmus here wrongly added the words "of them which are being saved" - from an uninspired comment on the Biblical text made by the A.D. 614 Andreas of Caesarea. This has done inestimable damage - in the hands of defeatistic 'Pessimillennialists.'

Other Works by Rev. Prof. Dr. Francis Nigel Lee

King Alfred the Great and our Common Law
The famous German Church Historian Rev. Professor Dr.J.H. Kurtz called King Alfred the greatest and noblest of all the monarchs England has ever had. King Alfred applied all the energy of his mind to the difficult problems of government; to the emancipation of his Christian country by driving out the Pagan Danish invaders and robbers; and then to improving the internal condition of the land. Alfred is perhaps best of all remembered for his famous Law Code. King Alfred's Book of Laws or Dooms came forth from the laws of Kent, Mercia and Wessex. All these attempted to blend the Mosaic Code with the Christian principles of Celto-Brythonic Law and old Germanic customs... the laws of Alfred, continually amplified by his successors, grew into that body of Customary Law which was administered as the 'Common Law' by the Shire and the Hundred Courts.

6th-Century Christian Britain from King Arthur to Rome's Austin

Prof. Dr. F.N. Lee first presents early evidence for the historicity of Arthur, the Celto-Brythonic 'High King' of Britain. Arthur established his presence in Ireland, Iceland, Dalriada, Pictavia, Norway and perhaps even elsewhere in Northern Europe. He also took a strong position against Rome, and refused all payment of tribute to that imperial(istic) city. Arthur defeated the Saxons in twelve major battles -- culminating in his own great heroism at Mt. Badon in A.D. 516. From this starting point in the time of Arthur, Prof. Dr. F.N. Lee takes us on a fascinating survey of sixth century Christian Britain, and the various personalities, and peoples that who dominated the times.

The Godly life of John Calvin
The Protestant Reformation had not yet begun. Yet the Dark Ages of many centuries of ignorance were about to end. For the art of printing had recently been invented. So the available number of Bibles was now steadily increasing. And the deepening study of that book, was clearly exposing the corruption of the Church. In this book Dr Lee gives a simple but practical account of the life of Calvin.

Visit www.BexleyPublications.co.uk to purchase any of these books.

www.ingramcontent.com/pod-product-compliance
Ingram Content Group UK Ltd.
Pitfield, Milton Keynes, MK11 3LW, UK
UKHW041903190726
13854UKWH00003B/1064